She probably adores me.

How corny.

100 WAYS TO AMAZE A KID

Collected by Kate Campbell
Illustrated by Erkki Alanen

LEXIKOS
San Francisco

Manufactured in the United States of America

Library of Congress Catalogue Card Number 82-81464

ISBN 0-938530-08-9

10 9 8 7 6 5 4 3

Amazing a kid, or entertaining a child, isn't difficult. Kids are eager to be entertained by adults. But some adults may feel they just don't know what to do; they feel tongue-tied and helpless when left alone with a child they don't know. This book is especially for them, but it's also for people who hang out with kids a lot and who want to expand their repertoire of tricks and twisters and the clever things that kids like.

Some of these tricks and riddles and amusements have been popular for generations. Others are newer inventions. You are sure to see some you remember from when you were a kid--but are glad to see again (like the rules for playing "Battleships").

We think the best way to amaze a kid is by amazing yourself first, with an unabashed willingness to make a fool of yourself. The most important thing is: Don't be afraid to. . . well, be a child for a while. Kids love it when adults come down from their age and height and maturity, do the unexpected, act a little nutty.

So, uncles and babysitters, grandmothers and old school buddies, all of you tossed into the company of demanding little folks, here are 100 ways to amaze a kid.

Kate Campbell

who collected the ways

MUNCH YOUR FINGER

Put a piece of carrot secretly in your mouth.
Then, announce that you're going to snack on
your finger. Feed it slowly into the side of your
mouth as you crunch down on the carrot.
A carrot has the best sound, but macaroni or
an ice cube work well, too.

THE GREAT NOSE ROBBERY

Quickly "nip" the kid's nose with your thumb and index finger while exclaiming, "Whoops! I've got your nose!"

Slip the tip of your thumb between two fingers and show him his "nose."

LAUGH GETTER No. 1

Cross your little finger over your ring finger,
then cross that over your middle finger; then
cross all three over the index finger. Do the
same with your other hand. Wave them in the
air and smile foolishly.

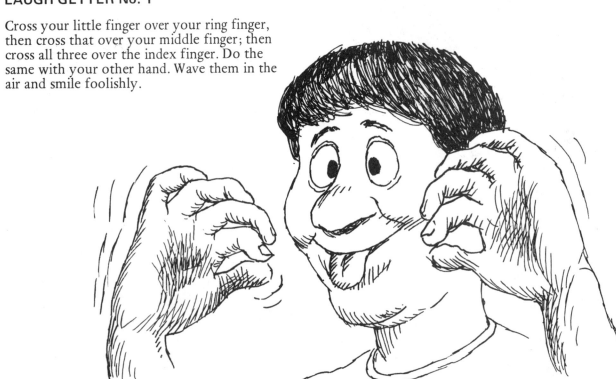

LAUGHING MOSQUITOES

Ask two kids to touch foreheads, close their eyes, and cross them. When you yell "Mosquitoes!" both kids should open their eyes and try to keep from laughing.

RIDDLE No. 1

What can you hold in your left hand but not in your right?

(Answer at the end of the book.)

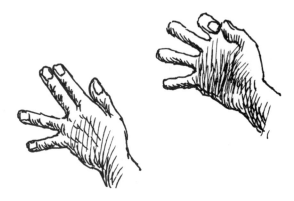

FRANKENSTEIN FINGERS

Holding an invisible "needle" in one hand and equally invisible "thread" in the other, pretend to thread the needle. Then, beginning with the index finger, pantomime a complete sewing job. Be serious and concentrate hard. As you sew each finger, pull the thread tight, making the fingers already sewn jerk together. Keep calm, remain pokerfaced. Continue sewing up to your elbow, then pull on the thread, making your hand wave at the kid.

REMOVABLE THUMB

Place your thumbs together as shown, and with your index finger cover the joint where the thumbs meet. When the right hand moves to the right, it appears to have the tip of the thumb under the right index finger.

Before you pull off your thumb tip, wiggle it to show the kid that it's real. Remove your thumb, showing concentrated effort and employing your best imitation of pain. Rejoin your thumb, and let the amazed kid examine it.

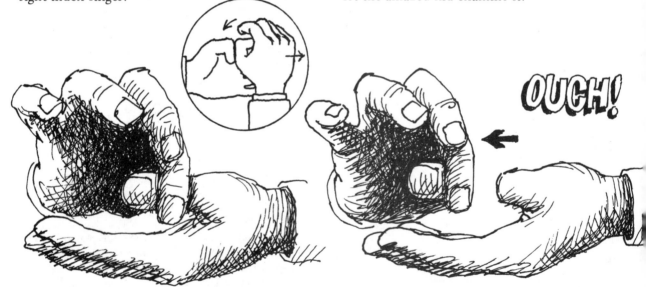

OUCH!

BREAK YOUR NOSE

Announce grandly that you'll break your nose. Place your hands on both sides of your nose. Put your thumbnail in a flicking position behind one of your front teeth so that the kid doesn't see it. Twist your hands to one side violently, while flicking your thumbnail so that a loud CRACK! can be heard. Be sure to unbreak your nose before removing your hands, unless your nose falls naturally to one side.

NO DUMMY, DUMMY

Draw a face on your hand as shown. By wiggling the middle of your thumb, you can make your hand talk.

RIDDLE No. 2

What weighs more, a pound of feathers or a pound of lead?

(Answer at the end of the book.)

THE CLASSIC WHISTLE

Stick your index and middle fingers in your mouth, one on each side, and blow air through. Everyone's technique differs slightly, but with practice, this is one of the world's loudest whistles. Keep this in mind if you decide to teach a kid to do this.

GRASS WHISTLE

Place a blade of grass or a thin strip of cellophane or paper lengthwise between your thumbs. Blow through it. The blade or strip will vibrate from the air and squeal. Like whistling through your fingers, this whistle can be very loud.

SNAPPING AS A SKILL

Teach the kid to snap his fingers. Someone has to!

GET IT RIGHT AND YOU'LL FLY

Ask the kid to revolve her arms in opposite directions.

WHICH DIGIT?

Have the kid fold her hands and squeeze them tight for about 10 seconds. Then point to one of the middle fingers or the ring finger and ask her to lift only that finger. She will probably lift the wrong one. If you think this is easy, have her do it to you.

NUMB, CREEPY FINGER

Hold up one hand palm to palm with the kid. Take turns running the thumb and index finger (of the other hand) up and down the side of the ring fingers being held up. It will feel like one side of your finger is numb, but it's really the other person's finger you are feeling.

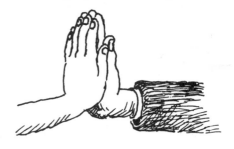

RAISE ONE EYEBROW WITHOUT SQUINTING

Then raise the other.

MIDDLE FINGER WAG

Hold your palms together, cross the middle
fingers, then reverse your palms so that the
middle fingers stick out. Waggle them.

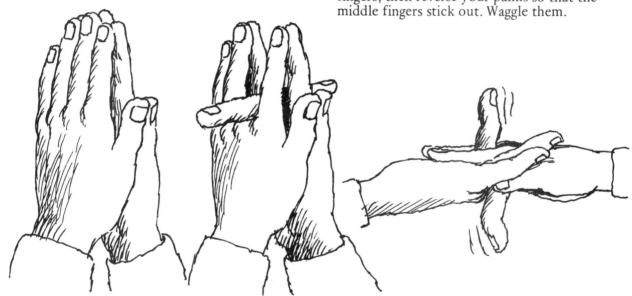

TOO MANY FINGERS

Taking the kid's hands, show him that he has 11 fingers by saying: "Here, I'll show you. And to prove it, we'll count backwards from 10." Point to each finger, "10, 9, 8, 7, 6" --then point to his other hand--"plus 5 equals 11!"

RIDDLE No. 3

What is black and white and red all over?

(Answer at the end of the book.)

THE DUMB THUMB

Kids do not appreciate this one at first, but they love to bug everybody else with it.

Using your thumb, point up, down, and around while saying:

Look up
Look down
See my thumb?
Gee you're dumb.

If a kid does this to you, at least you'll know what's coming.

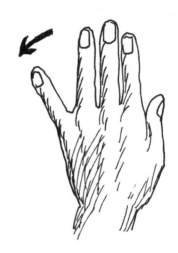

MORE FINGER FUN

Hold your hand up, fingers together. Beginning with the thumb, split your fingers one by one-- first, the index finger and the thumb, then the index finger, middle finger, and the thumb, and so on, until you reach the little finger. Do it again, starting with the little finger. Did you do it without effort?

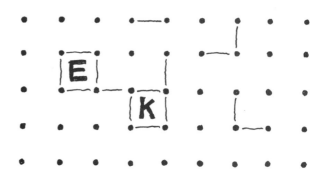

THE BODY'S WILLING BUT...

Rest your fingers on a table as shown in the illustration. Raise two fingers at a time, returning them to the table: Lift 1 and 2 together, then 3 and 4, then 1 and 4, and 2 and 3. Now try to raise 1 and 3, then 2 and 4. It's harder than it sounds.

PAPER FEAT

Bet a kid that he can't fold a piece of paper in half more than nine times. He can use any kind of paper. Rest assured, you'll win the bet.

A PRETTY SQUARE GAME

Draw a grid of dots in lines and columns. You can draw as many dots as you like, or you can use graph paper and put the dots on intersecting lines, a few squares apart.

The object of the game is to complete boxes by drawing one line on a turn, only between two dots. The player who completes a box by drawing the last side "owns" the box, and puts his initial in it. Rule: A box may have only four dots, no more. The winner is the player with the largest number of boxes when all possible lines have been drawn.

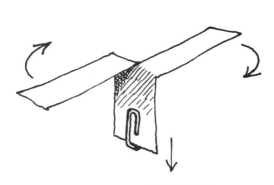

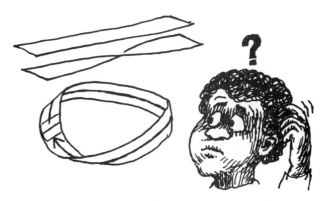

THE WRIGHT BROTHERS SPECIAL

Cut a strip of paper about 8 inches long or so and about an inch wide. Make a slit halfway down the middle, fold the split pieces in opposite directions, and put a paper clip on the un-split bottom as shown in the illustration. Have the kids drop it straight and it will whirl like a helicopter.

RIDDLE No. 4

What do you call a cat that just ate a pickle?

(Answer at the end of the book.)

MYSTERIOUS MOBIUS

Tear a strip of paper about 1 inch wide and 8½ inches long. Show that the paper has two sides. Then twist one end one-half a turn and attach the ends with tape to form a loop.

Show the kid how one side of the paper seems to have disappeared by drawing a line through the middle of the strip, and--surprise, the line will meet itself!

A M A Z _ _ G

GRISLY, BUT FUN

This is an old game and is played in several countries. In France it's called "le pendu."

Draw the scaffolding as shown. Think of a word and, next to the scaffold, draw a short line for each letter. The kid must guess the letters in your word. If he guesses A, for example, you must fill in all the A's that appear in the word. For each letter guessed that's not in the word, draw in part of the hangman's body. If the figure is complete before the kid guesses your word, you, the executioner, win. (You can give the kid a break--or prolong the agony--by drawing hands, fingers, toes, and face.)

HOW WELL CAN YOU READ?

AN
AN APPLE A
A DAY KEEPS THE
THE DOCTOR AWAY

What does this really say? Ask the child to read it
it without making any mistakes. (Little kids may
read it more correctly than an older kid who
already "knows" what it says.)

RIDDLE No. 5

What is it that has ears like a cat, a head like a
cat, feet like a cat, a tail like a cat, but isn't a cat?

(Answer at the end of the book.)

SOLAR POWER DOESN'T COUNT

You can draw the three houses and the three
utilities--water, electricity, and gas--in any form
you like. The object is to connect each of the
houses with each of the utilities without cross-
ing any of the lines. Give up?

(Answer at the end of the book.)

HOLY PALM

Roll up a piece of paper into a tube, and have the kid hold it up to one eye, leaving both eyes open. Have him hold up the other hand, in front of the hand holding the tube, with the palm facing him. It will look like there is a hole in his palm!

JUST DON'T USE A DISHWASHER

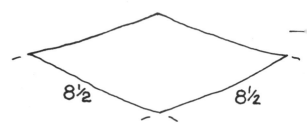

Take a square piece of paper about 8½ x 8½ inches or so (you can cut the extra 2½ inches off a sheet of regular typing paper).

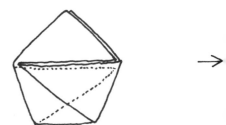

Turn the paper over and do the same to this side, making sure that the top edges are even on both sides.

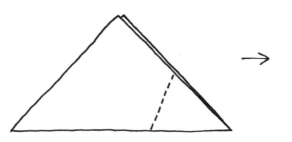

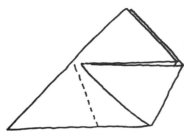

Fold up one point of the square to make a tri-
angle. Make sure the fold is on the bottom.

Fold the right point over to the middle of the
opposite edge.

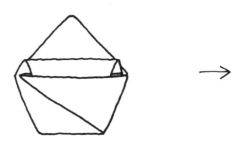

If you think the kid is going to want to drink
out of the cup, institute a little game to see who
can drink faster (the cup will leak after a while).

RIDDLE No. 6

Who wears a coat all winter and pants in the summer?

(Answer at the end of the book.)

PICASSO COULDN'T DO IT

Ask the kid to draw the envelope below, without lifting the pen from the paper or retracing any lines.

(Answer at the end of the book.)

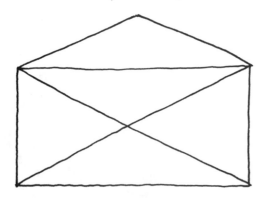

THREE-PERSON TIC-TAC-TOE

This game is played the same as Tic-Tac-Toe except that a grid of three horizontal lines and three vertical lines is used. Each player chooses a letter, and the first one to get three letters in a row wins.

Some people play with the additional rule that all of the outside squares must be filled in before the inside squares.

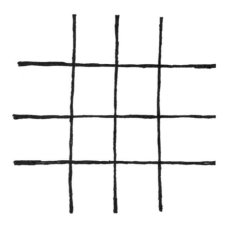

MY FLEA, YOU SEE

Place a pencil under the edge of a piece of paper, holding the paper low and the pencil lightly by the eraser, so that the kids don't see it. Tell the kids that you have an incredible, trained, jumping flea that will jump on command. Demand that the "flea" jump, then follow it with your eyes. When it "lands" tap the under-side of the paper slightly with the pencil.

IT'S EASIER THAN ASTROLOGY

With the following arithmetic, you can amaze a kid by being able to accurately "guess" her age and birthdate.

Without your looking, have her write down the number of the month and day of her birth as a single number. For example, October 24 would be 1024. Then have her do the following:

1. Multiply the number by 2.
2. Add 5.
3. Multiply by 50.
4. Then add her age.

Now ask her to tell you the final number, which looks long and confused. Write it down; look at it intently; press your fingers to your temple; knit your brow. Then like a wizard, announce you've divined the answer. "You were born October 24 and you're 9 years old!" Here's how to do it: Subtract 250 and determine her birth-date and age from the number that's left:

102409

10 is the month of her birth; 24 is the day; 09 is her age.

RIDDLE No. 7

How far can you go into the woods?

(Answer at the end of the book.)

SNOWFLAKES

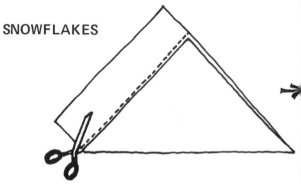

Take a piece of regular 8½ x 11 typing paper and make it square by folding and cutting it as shown.

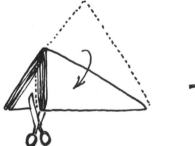

Fold the top point down as shown, and cut along the dotted line.

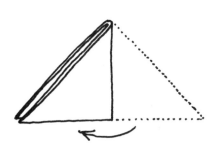

Fold the right point over to the left.

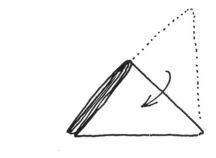

Fold the top point down to the left.

Now have the kid make cuts on all the edges, but leaving some of the fold remaining on each side. The more paper that's carefully cut away, the lacier the snowflake will look unfolded.

Next they'll probably try to make me out of paper!

BATTLESHIPS

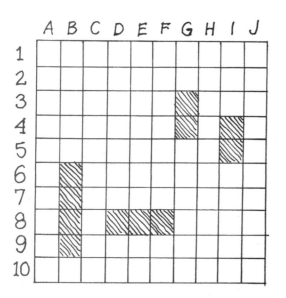

Make two grids, as shown in the illustration, one for each player. You can have any number of boxes, but 100 is standard. Each player gets:

    1 battleship--four boxes long
    1 cruiser--three boxes long
    2 destroyers--two boxes long

Or any other variation that you and the other player decide upon.

The object of the game is to sink all of the other player's ships. Each player decides where to put her ships on the grid, and shades in the appropriate boxes so that the other player doesn't see.

Each square must be named by letter and number to score a hit. Four squares must be named to sink a battleship, for example. At the start of the game, one player calls out four boxes. The other player then says whether any ships have been hit, naming the location. Then she gets her turn to fire.

Mark the boxes differently so you can see which shots you fired and which ones were hits.

When a player loses a ship, she can fire one less shot on a turn. For example, if a player has lost both a destroyer and the battleship, she gets only two calls on a turn.

POOR MAN'S MOVIE

Seen in rapid succession a series of still pictures appear animated to the human eye. This fact makes movies possible.

You can have a kid make his own moving picture. Staple a bunch of paper together or use a notepad. Have him draw pictures of moving figures such as a person running, or a dog, or a horse. When the papers are flipped quickly, the figure moves.

FLYING STRAW

Cut two strips of fairly thick paper, about 1 inch wide and 3 inches long. Tape the ends to form loops and tape each loop to the ends of a drinking straw. Toss it and watch it fly!

THE IMPOSSIBLE OMELETTE

Have the kid hold an egg in his hands as shown. Ask him to try to break the egg by applying equal pressure to the tips of the egg. If you are a coward, use a boiled egg. There is less of a mess in case of an accident.

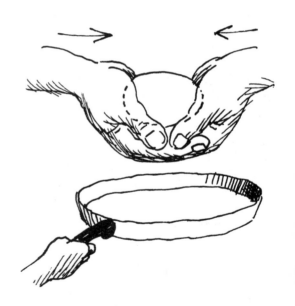

EGG ON END

When no one is looking, moisten the wide end
of an egg and roll it in a little salt. The salt crystals will stick to the egg, allowing it to stand up
on end.

OR, WAIT FOR THE BLUE MOON

We've been told that it's possible to balance an egg without salt, but only on the spring and fall equinox. This may be because the earth's poles are the same distance away from the sun on the equinox. If it's not the equinox and you don't have any salt, however, try balancing the egg on a cloth-covered table. This sometimes works.

RIDDLE No. 8

What did Delaware? What did Tennessee? What did Idaho?

(Answers at the end of the book.)

JUST DON'T DRINK IT

Pour some salt out onto a napkin, put some pepper on it, and mix it all up. Ask the kids how long they think it would take to separate the salt from the pepper, and how it could be done.

Pour the mixture in a glass of water. The salt will sink and the pepper will float, separating one from the other instantly.

MAKE A SNAKE

Tear open one end of a paper-wrapped straw, squeezing the paper together like an accordion at the other end. Put the wrapper in some water in a saucer and watch it uncoil like a snake.

THE MAGNETIC SALT SHAKER

Insert a toothpick or a wooden match in one of
the holes in a salt shaker. Conceal the toothpick
with your finger and lift the shaker.

EFFORTLESS ICE CUBE LIFT

Hand a piece of string to a kid and ask him to take an ice cube out of the water with the string. Unless he thinks of it first, you can do it by lowering one end of the string onto the ice cube, making a small loop with it. Sprinkle some salt on the cube and the string. Wait until the string has stuck, and pull the cube out of the glass!

THE AMAZING SHRINKING LIQUID

If you pour one cup of rubbing alcohol into one cup of water, how much liquid will you have?

About a cup and three-quarters, depending upon the strength of the alcohol. The water absorbs the alcohol. The larger the quantity of water and alcohol, the more dramatic the results will be. Use a measuring cup to show this bit of magic more clearly.

EENY-MEENY, MIGHTY ODD

Like flipping a coin, "shooting fingers" is used to decide something. Each player chooses "evens" or "odds." They then "shoot" or thrust the fingers of one hand from an upraised fist at the same time. They may shoot as many fingers as they like (1 to 4). If the sum of all fingers both players shoot is odd, the player who chose "odds" wins. If the sum is even, the one who chose "evens" wins. Usually when deciding an issue or choosing sides for a game, the winner of 2 out of 3 "shoots" wins.

SCISSORS, PAPER, STONE

This is an old game for two players, similar to
the one on the previous page. Each player
throws at the same time:

    Two fingers in a V are scissors;
    An open palm is paper;
    A fist is stone.

Scissors win over paper because scissors can cut
paper. Paper wins over stone because paper can
be wrapped around a stone. A stone wins over
scissors because stone blunts scissors.

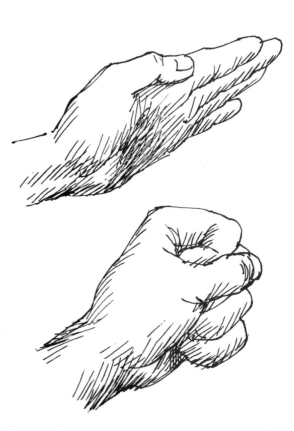

(DON'T) CLAP YOUR NOSE

Have a kid touch his ear with the opposite hand, and touch his nose with the other hand, clap, and then reverse his hands, as quickly as possible.

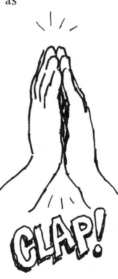

CRAZYLEGS REVISITED

Remember the Charleston? Even if you never learned any steps, you can teach a kid that famous hands-on-your-knees move:

Stand with your knees apart and bent, left hand on left knee, right hand on right knee. Bring your knees together and cross your hands, putting your left hand on your right knee and your right hand on your left knee. Spread your knees apart again, leaving your hands on the opposite knee. Bring your knees together, uncrossing your hands and spread your knees apart again. Do it over and over, making your movements quick and smooth.

PLEASE REMAIN SEATED

Have a kid sit in a chair as shown in the illustration. Tell him that you are a powerful hypnotist and with just one finger, you can prevent him from getting up from the chair.

Put your finger on his forehead, applying slight downward pressure. Tell him to get up. He won't be able to until he lifts his head, which you are preventing with just one finger pushing on his forehead.

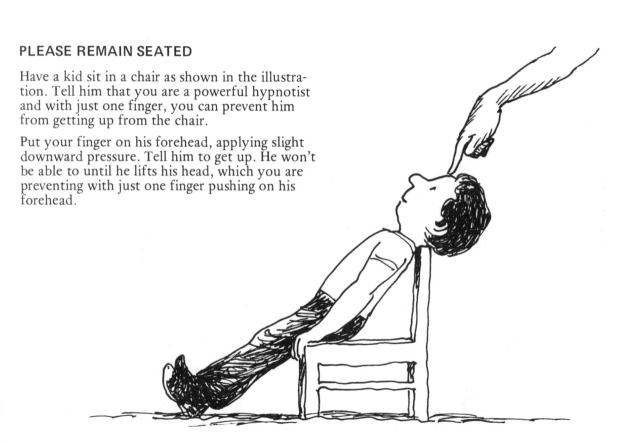

HUMAN ELEVATOR

Ask the child to hold her arms very stiffly at her sides, with her fists clenched. Lift her carefully, by cupping your hands under her fists. This won't work unless she holds her arms very stiffly.

"X" MARKS THE SPOT

On the kid's back, trace a big X, a zero, and a dot while saying, "X marks the spot, with a zero, and a dot," then quickly reach up and gently squeeze the back of his neck saying, "get the chills?" If this is done quickly, he will indeed feel a light shiver up the spine. Or perhaps the mere suggestion makes it work.

Here's a follow-up:
Take turns tracing out letters on each other's back. If the kid is old enough, trace out a message, one letter at a time.

HOW TO DRIVE A KID BATTY

Leave the room and rush back in, holding your hands in a cup and discreetly clicking your nail against another, wiggling your hands slightly as you do it. Announce with trepidation that you'v caught a bat. If you can enlist someone else to join the conspiracy, pass the "bat" to him. Whe the time is right, pass the bat to the kid.

SHAKE IT OUT

If the child is small, pick him up by the waist and flip him gently upside-down. Shake him a little and say, "We have to shake it all out! Is it all out, yet?" As long as he hasn't had enough, you can bet that the answer will be a resounding, "NO!" This is a great trick to turn a tired, moody toddler into a non-stop giggler.

THE NONVIOLENT EGG

Sneak up behind a kid and tell her you're going to break an egg over her head. Before she has a chance to turn around, rest your fist on top of her head, then hit your fist with the flat side of your other hand, making a loud CRACK! Un-curl your fist slowly, spreading your fingers down over her head. It'll feel like a gooey egg.

OUR FRIEND GRAVITY

Have a kid stand against the wall as shown, so that the side of one foot is against the baseboard. Now ask her to raise the other foot. Without falling.

IT'S A LITTLE EASIER THAN RUBBER BABY RUGGY GUMPERS

Rub your stomach and pat your head at the same time.

WHERE'S OUR FRIEND GRAVITY NOW?

Ask a kid to stand in a doorway as shown, pushing the backs of his hands against the door-frame, concentrating for 15 seconds or so on pushing the doorframe away from him. Ask him to stand away from the doorway. His arms will magically rise by themselves!

PRETEND YOU'RE A ROBOT

THOITY DOITY POIPLE BOIDS

Teach a kid a funny verse:

Thoity doity poiple boids sittin awn a coibstone,
choipin and boipin;
Along comes Goidy and his friend Moity,
When THEY saw thoity doity poiple boids
sittin awn the coibstone, choipin and boipin;
BOY! Where THEY pertoibed!!

WADJA EXPECT!

Tell him that if he can rip a paper napkin into
four equal pieces, you'll give him a quarter.
Examine the pieces carefully, then hand one
back to him and say, "Here's your quarter."

ANYTHING BUT MASHED POTATOES

Hold one hand under the table and take a dinner
roll in the other hand. Exclaim that your roll is
too hard to eat. Prove it by slapping the roll
down while hitting the underside of the table
with your knuckle. Ask the kid to slap her roll
down on the table. When it doesn't make a
sound, ask her for it. Slap it down on the table,
again hitting the underside with your knuckle.

THREE-PENNY PINCH

Drop three pennies onto the end of a table. The object of the game is to shoot the penny closest to the edge of the table between the other two pennies by flicking it with the index finger. The pennies must not hit each other and if they do, it's the other player's turn. Players score one point each time they successfully flick one penny between the other two without touching them. The penny closest to the starting edge of the table is always used as the "shooter" penny, and the game progresses until the other end of the table is reached.

DISAPPEARING DIME

This trick requires a dime and a matchbox. Dump out the matches and put in the dime. Shake the box up and down and sideways and all around, announcing that you're going to make the dime disappear. As you shake the box, turn it over momentarily and press the sides in; the arch should allow the dime to fall out into your hand without anyone's seeing it. Put the box on the table. Tell the kid to stare at the box while you say your magic. Say anything that sounds magical, slipping the dime into your pocket while the kid stares at the box. Tell the kid to open the box.

CRYSTAL CLEAR

This works best with a crystal wine glass, but it will also work on some regular glasses with separate stems: Wet your finger and run it around the rim of the glass. The friction creates an eerie, penetrating squeal.

MATCH THAT!

Count out 9 wooden matches. Ask the kid if those 9 matches could be made into 10 in any way. Use 2 matches to make a "T," 4 matches to make an "E," and 3 matches to make an "N."

Then ask him if 10 can be made out of 5 matches. Use 1 match to make a "1" and 4 matches to make a square "0."

If you make it this far, ask him if 2 matches could be made into 10. Use 2 matches to make Roman numeral X.

Then tell the kid that you can make 1 match into 10. Let him ponder this for a while, then pick up the match, put it into your pocket, and drop a dime onto the table. Give him the dime for putting up with you.

NAME THAT TUNE

Have a kid tap out a tune on a glass (lightly!) and see if you can guess what it is.

ONE OF LIFE'S LITTLE LESSONS

When a kid wants to flip a coin to decide an issue, say quickly, "Heads I win, tails you lose." This works only once in life.

GOOD BET

There are 10 possible numbers (0 to 9) in an 8-digit serial number on a dollar bill. Bet a kid that you can quess at least one of the numbers with just two guesses. The odds are 5 to 1 that you can.

SHRINKING DOLLAR

Scrunch up a dollar bill into a tight ball and knead it in your hands. Flatten out the bill but don't smooth out the wrinkles. The bill will look like it has shrunk. If you scrunch it up and smooth it out once more, it will look even smaller.

RIDDLE No. 9

What kinds of animals can jump higher than a house?

(Answer at the end of the book.)

MATCHED SQUARES

Put four wooden matches on a table exactly as you see them here. Ask the kid to make a square by moving only one match.

Pull the top match upwards slightly so that the end of it is even with the two horizontal matches, making a tiny square in the center.

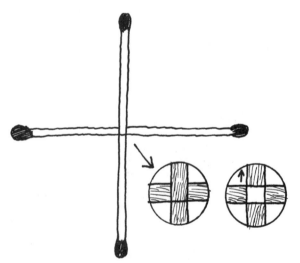

HERE'S MY CARD

This trick requires a business card, a nickel, and some practice. Put a business card and a nickel on your finger as shown. Make sure that the nickel is over the first joint of your finger. By sharply flicking the edge of the card, you can make it fly out from under the nickel, without moving the nickel.

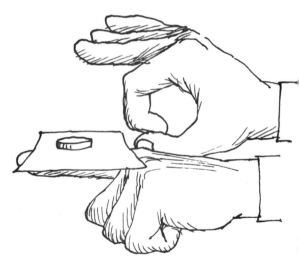

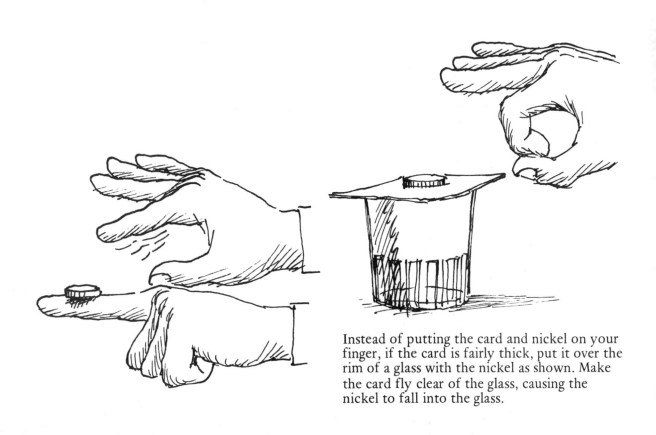

Instead of putting the card and nickel on your finger, if the card is fairly thick, put it over the rim of a glass with the nickel as shown. Make the card fly clear of the glass, causing the nickel to fall into the glass.

NEXT STOP, STANFORD BUSINESS SCHOOL

Bet the kid that he can't catch a dollar bill with his index finger and thumb. Have him hold his hand just below the bottom edge of the bill as shown. Drop the bill straight. It is just a little too short to catch unless he has very quick reflexes.

WHO SAYS IT'S UNLUCKY?!

There are no fewer than 8 symbols on the Seal of the United States, on the back of a dollar bill, that have 13 things in them:

13 letters in "E Pluribus Unum"
13 stars in the halo
13 clouds to form the halo
13 stripes in the shield
13 arrows in one claw
13 leaves on the branch
13 berries on the branch
13 feathers on the eagle's neck.

THE FATHER OF OUR SALAD

Fold a dollar bill lengthwise so that Washington's eyes are just below the fold. Make another lengthwise fold (slightly crooked) so that his eyes are folded downward to his chin. Take a look at him now!

THE FLEEING COIN

Line up three coins, touching each other. With
an index finger, press down hard on the middle
coin, then move one of the outer coins away
and strike it against the edge of the middle coin.
The coin you didn't touch will move "by itself,"
from transmitted shock.

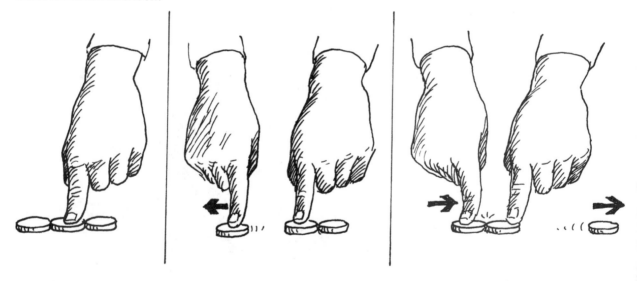

LADIES AND GENTS

Ladies and gents and dogs without fleas;
Cover your ears and listen up please!
I come here before you to stand here behind you,
to tell a story I know nothing about.
The admission is free so pay at the door,
pull up a chair and sit on the floor.
One dark night in broad daylight,
two dead men decided to fight.
Back to back and facing each other,
they pulled out their swords and shot one another.
A deaf policeman heard the noise
and came to arrest the two dead boys.
Ask the blindman, he saw it, too.

SUGAR ROCKS

This trick needs some time to perform. Dissolve as much sugar as you can in a small amount of water in a cup. Suspend a string in the cup, tying the top around a pencil to keep the string away from the edge of the cup. Put the cup in a breezy or sunny window and wait several days until most of the water has evaporated. Then pull the string out of the cup. Crystals will have formed on the string, making "rocks" of sugar.

THE WORLD'S BEST TONGUE-TWISTERS

A skunk sat on a stump.
The skunk thunk the stump stunk,
and the stump thunk the skunk stunk.

*

Rubber baby buggy bumpers,
rubber baby buggy bumpers...

RIDDLE No. 10

The King asked his blind servant to get him a pair of socks. The blind servant knows that the King has 20 pairs of white socks and 20 pairs of black socks all mixed up in his drawer. What's the fewest number of socks the blind servant must bring back to the King to be sure that he has a matched pair?

(Answer at the end of the book.)

ELBOW CATCH

Put a coin (or if you're ambitious, a stack of
coins) on your elbow. Flip your elbow and catch
the coins.

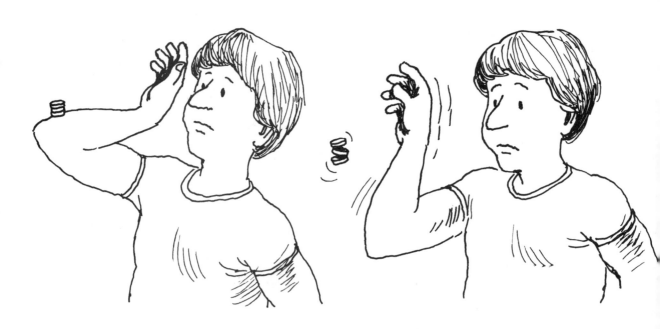

THE UNLEANING TOWER

Roll up 4 sheets of paper all the same size -- about the size of this book. Put a rubber band or tape around the tubes, without crimping the tubes. Carefully, put a book (start with a large, light one) on the ends as shown, then another and another. You'll be amazed at how many books these paper pillars can hold. As soon as the weight isn't distributed evenly, however, you'll create a "structural stress," and the pile will topple.

All right, now tell me how to get down.

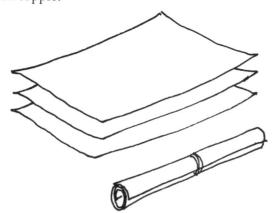

WRINKLES FOR STRENGTH

This demonstration shows another basic principle of construction -- that corrugated building materials are stronger than flat materials. You need three short glasses and a piece of large paper. To show how weak a flat surface is, try to put the third glass on top of the paper. Take the paper and fold it up like an accordion, making as many folds as you can. The paper is now able to support the weight of the glass.

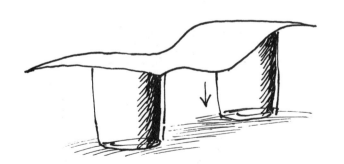

THAT OLD SINKING FEELING

Take a soda bottle and **3** paper matchheads.
Fill the bottle completely with water. Put the
matchheads in the bottle. They'll float. Now
put your thumb on the mouth of the bottle
and press down. Presto! The matcheads begin
to sink. They'll stop at different levels. The
smaller the head, the lower it sinks.

The matchheads sink because the water pressure,
generated by your thumb, forces air out of the
heads. The moral? There is none.

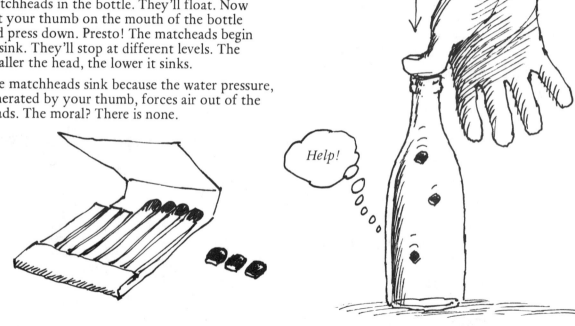

Help!

GREENBACK SNATCH

For this you need two bottles and a fresh buck.
Arrange the bottles and a crisp dollar bill as
shown. Make sure that the rims of the bottles
match exactly.

Hold one end of the bill taut, and sharply snap
the bill out with you other hand.

Once you've mastered this, go for the tablecloth!

GHOSTLY GAME

Pretend suddenly that the kid is invisible. Ask
everybody in the room if they've seen or heard
her. Of course, no one will have. "Gee, maybe
she's invisible!" Start talking about her, about
her birthday or Christmas, but just when you're
about to say what she's going to be getting,
pretend that she's no longer invisible.

SUNDIAL

You can use a pencil poked through a paper plate or simply a stick, as shown. Mark the time that you and the kid made the sundial by putting a mark on the paper plate or by putting another stick where the shadow falls. Decide on a time when you will come back, estimate where the shadow will fall at that time, and mark the spot. Return at the decided-upon time and see where the shadow falls. How close did you come to predicting where the sun would be?

GRAB BAG

Put an assortment of common and interesting items into a bag or pillowcase. Have the kid guess what's in the bag by reaching in and feeling the items.

TAKE IT OFF!!

Get a blanket and put it in the middle of the floor. Tell the kid to crawl under the blanket and take off something he doesn't need. As the shoes and clothing appear from under the blanket, tell him he still hasn't taken off what he needs the least. When he's taken off enough to get him ready for bed, inform him that the thing he needed least in the first place was the blanket. Grab him quickly and carry him off to bed.

ANSWERS

Riddles:

No. 1. Your right elbow.

No. 2. They both weigh the same--one pound.

No. 3. An embarrassed zebra. Or a newspaper.

No. 4. A sourpuss.

No. 5. A kitten.

No. 6. A dog.

No. 7. Only halfway. The other half, you're coming out, not going in.

No. 8. What did Delaware? A New Jersey.
What did Tennessee? She saw what Arkansas.
What did Idaho? I don't know, but Alaska.

No. 9. All kinds. Houses can't jump.

No. 10. The servant must bring back three socks to the King. At least two of them will be white or two will be black, giving the King a matched pair.

Three houses, three utilities:

There is no way, which shouldn't amaze people who pay utility bills.

The envelope drawing:

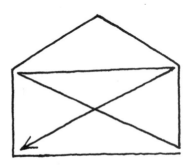

WHAT'S YOUR FAVORITE WAY TO AMAZE A KID?

Tell us about it. If we decide to put it in ANOTHER 100 WAYS TO AMAZE A KID, we'll send you a free copy of the book and credit you with the trick. (One book per entrant.)

Please describe your trick as clearly as possible, including a rough sketch (if necessary), to help us understand exactly how it should be done.

Then tear out this page and fold it as instructed on the back.

(We've also included ordering information for more copies of 100 WAYS TO AMAZE A KID.)

Here's my trick and how it's done:

_____

_____

_____

_____

_____

_____

Please send____more copies of 100 WAYS TO AMAZE A KID (@ $3.95 + $1.50 for postage and handling; California residents add applicable sales tax).

Name: _____

Address: _____

_____

_____

Fold here and staple or tape edge

Kate Campbell
"Amaze a Kid" Department
LEXIKOS
4079 19th Ave.
San Francisco, CA 94132

Cut here